ROLLER COASTERS

ROLLER COASTERS

ROLLER COASTERS
or I Had So Much Fun, I Almost Puked

by Nick Cook

 Carolrhoda Books, Inc./Minneapolis

To Dori. Thanks for pointing the way.

The publisher would like to thank Dr. Robert Cartmell, Randy Geisler, Paul L. Ruben, and the staff of the Valleyfair Family Amusement Park in Shakopee, Minnesota.

Text copyright © 1998 by Nick Cook

All rights reserved. International copyright secured. No part of this book may be reproduced, stored in a retrieval system, or transmitted in any form or by any means, electronic, mechanical, photocopying, recording, or otherwise, without the prior written permission of Carolrhoda Books, Inc., except for the inclusion of brief quotations in an acknowledged review.

Carolrhoda Books, Inc., c/o The Lerner Publishing Group
241 First Avenue North, Minneapolis, MN 55401 U.S.A.

Website address: www.lernerbooks.com

LIBRARY OF CONGRESS CATALOGING-IN-PUBLICATION

Cook, Nick, 1954–
   Roller coasters, or, I had so much fun, I almost puked / Nick Cook.
     p.   cm.
   Includes bibliographical references (p.) and index.
   Summary: Discusses the history, physics, parts, and design of roller coasters and examines some modern examples.
   ISBN 1-57505-071-4
   1. Roller coasters—Juvenile literature. [I. Roller coasters.] I. Title.
GV1860.R64C66 1998
791'.06'873—dc21   97-14394

Manufactured in the United States of America
Reprinted by arrangement with The Lerner Publishing Group.

10 9 8 7 6 5 4 3 2 1

Front cover: *Riders zoom by on the Wild Thing, a roller coaster at the Valleyfair Family Amusement Park in Shakopee, Minnesota.*
Back cover: *LaMarcus Adna Thompson built this roller coaster in Venice, California, in 1910.*
Page one: *The Giant Dipper glows on a moonlit night at Belmont Park in San Diego, California.*
Pages two and three: *The Windjammer roller coaster takes riders through a few loops at Knott's Berry Farm in Buena Park, California.*
Opposite page: *Roller coasters have been thrilling American riders for more than one hundred years.*

Metric Conversion Chart		
When You Know:	*Multiply by:*	*To Find:*
feet	.30	meters
miles	1.61	kilometers
pounds	0.45	kilograms

Contents

Chapter 1. Fear Rules the Rails	7
Chapter 2. Scream Machines	9
Chapter 3. These Dogs Don't Bark	23
Chapter 4. Curves, Corkscrews, and a Few G's	31
Chapter 5. Engineering, Psychology, plus a Little Courage	41
A Coaster Spotter's Guide	50
Glossary	54
Great Places to Look for More on Coasters	55
Index	56

Twists and turns make it hard to know what's coming next on this roller coaster ride.

Chapter 1

Fear Rules the Rails

You take a seat. The cars lurch out of the station. The chain grabs the first car and hoists the train up a steep hill. "Clank! Clank! Clank!" The train shudders and seems to drop backward. You look at the rails along the track. They seem awfully old. When was this thing built, you wonder, during the Civil War?

The first car reaches the top of the hill. For a second, the train perches at the first steep drop. Maybe this wasn't such a good idea, you think. The train hesitates, as if it's trying to make up its mind. Then the cars plunge.

The ground blurs. Your eyes water. Air stings your face. You try to remember to breathe. The train hits bottom and rockets up the next hill. You feel as if you left your stomach behind. You crest another hill. Back down you go, then suddenly you turn left. Right, up, down, left, down, up...

"AAAEEEIIIYYY!"

The cars brake suddenly and your screams die down. The train coasts into the station like a purring cat. The nightmare is over. And you think, Can I go again?

About three hundred million people ride roller coasters each year. Why? It's simple. They want to be scared to death. And they'll pay to do it.

People can climb Mount Everest to be scared. They can swim in shark-infested seas. The catch is that people want to be scared *and* be completely safe at the same time. Horror movies and scary books are popular for the same reason. Folks may be scared watching a movie or reading a book, but they realize the images and stories are fantasy. They can control the fright by closing their eyes or the book.

Roller coasters may look dangerous, but they're not. Riding a merry-go-round or just tripping hurts more people each year than do roller coaster rides. Roller coasters thrill people, scare them, and let them challenge death—safely.

The supports and beams of a wooden coaster may look rickety, but roller coasters are actually very safe.

Chapter 2

Scream Machines

By the 1600s and 1700s, ice slides were a common attraction in Russia.

Where did the bright idea to speed down a fake hill in a carriage start? The roller coaster's family tree begins in Russia in the 1400s or 1500s.

Ice sledding was a popular winter sport in Russia, and it was a big attraction during festivals. Seventy-foot hills were built out of wood. The hills sloped about as steeply as modern roller coasters. Hard-packed snow covered the wood frames. Spraying water on the snow and letting it freeze increased the hill's zip.

Guides took riders down the slope. The rider sat in the guide's lap on a two-foot-long sled. Anyone who wanted a repeat trip lugged the sled back up the hill. At slides outside Saint Petersburg, Russia, during the 1700s, colorful lanterns strung down the slope allowed night sledding. Russian empress Catherine the Great apparently enjoyed the sport. Once wheels were added to the sleds, she could ride during the warm months.

Ice slides came to France in the early 1800s. Changes were made since France's weather is milder than Russia's. Instead of sliding on snow, sleds coasted across closely spaced rollers, much like warehouse conveyors. (This may be where the term "roller coaster" originated.)

The first wheeled coaster opened in Paris in 1804. It was named Russian Mountains, after the home of the original sport. Small carriages followed metal tracks down a steep, wooden hill. Many carriages jumped the track and caused injuries. Even if the carriages stayed on course, sometimes riders tumbled out.

Opposite page: *Closely spaced rollers on the Russian Mountains in Paris may be where we get the term "roller coaster."*
Right: *Cars on the Aerial Walks headed down a steep hill before looping back up to the central tower.*

Despite these dangers, Parisians liked the Russian Mountains. Survivors of the first ride climbed a tower to the top of the hill for another try.

Another Paris coaster rose in the Beaujon Garden in 1817. The Aerial Walks showed much improvement over the first coaster. Guardrails lined the tracks to stop cars from hurtling over the edge. The coaster wasn't completely safe, however. The tracks had to be completely free of debris. One car hit a chestnut that lay on the tracks. The car upset, and the unlucky rider broke a leg.

On this coaster, two cars started on side-by-side tracks. At the bottom of a hill, the tracks separated and circled back to the station. The drop from the station usually gave the cars enough energy to carry the riders back to the start. (Workers sometimes had to give the cars a shove to return them to the station.) People bought a string of tickets. When they arrived back at the station, they simply handed the operator another ticket for another ride.

The French government granted a number of patents for roller coasters between 1817 and 1826. One inventor designed motors for the cars, powered by a machine like a windmill. Another inventor apparently wanted to give riders some exercise. He designed handrails for each side of the track so passengers could pull themselves uphill. Still another inventor suggested a game for his coaster. Riders were supposed to catch rings placed by the track...with spears. Even with all these innovations, the French seemed to tire of coasters after the mid-1800s. Soon development moved to the United States.

Trains, Planes, and Mules

The roller coaster arrived in North America, on paper at least, in the 1870s. J. G. Taylor and Richard Knudsen each received United States patents for inclined-plane railways. On Knudsen's ride, two side-by-side tracks ran between two towers. Gravity pulled the four-passenger cars down gently sloping hills. Elevators in the towers hauled the cars and riders up the opposite tower for the return trip. Neither Taylor nor Knudsen is believed to have actually built these rides, but mules in Pennsylvania already had a roller coaster all their own.

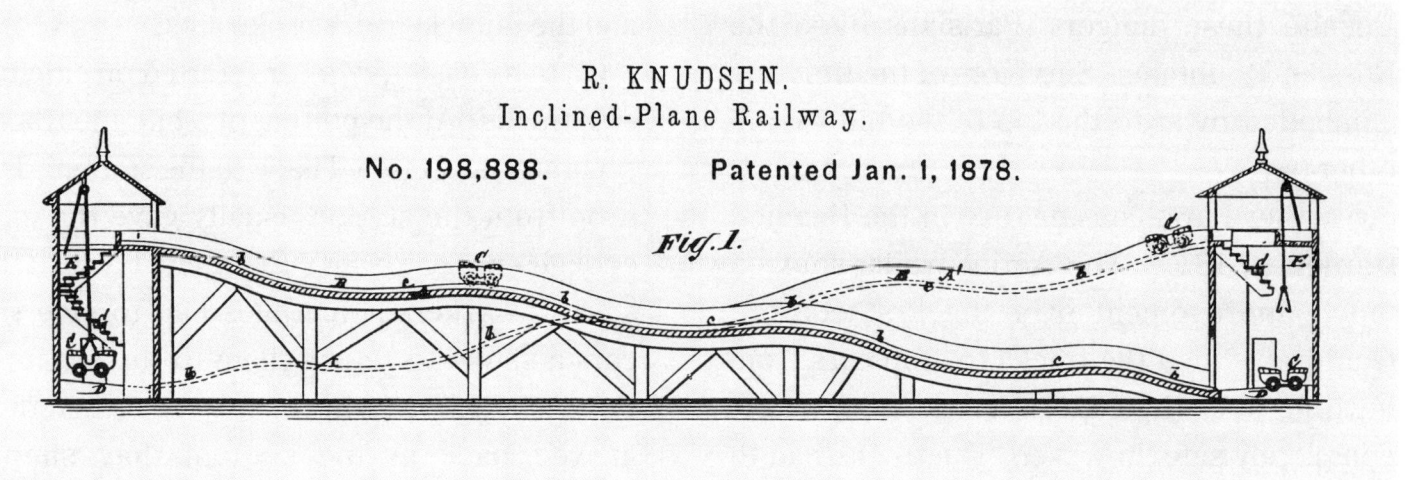

No one knows if Richard Knudsen built his inclined-plane railway, patented in 1878, but the ride clearly pointed the way to future roller coaster rides.

Once atop Mount Pisgah, passengers on the Mauch Chunk switchback railway enjoyed the view. Low booster wheels helped push cars up the steep slopes.

Near the town of Mauch Chunk (later renamed Jim Thorpe), a short railroad line hauled coal from the top of Mount Pisgah to a canal below. Mules drew the empty cars up the mountain, then boarded a special car. After the coal was loaded, the train—and the mules—coasted downhill to the canal. The railway, called a switchback, operated like this until the mine closed it in the early 1870s.

We don't know if the mules enjoyed the trip or not, but some Mauch Chunk citizens thought people would. The old mine train route reopened as a pleasure railroad. Passengers rode in a comfortable car. Steam engines pulled the car to the top of Mount Pisgah. Then the car glided down the slope like the old mine train it replaced. There were plenty of sights along the way. Riders viewed beautiful scenery. They also passed the amazing burning mine, on fire since 1832.

People flocked to the Mauch Chunk switchback railway. In 1873, thirty-five thousand visitors paid five cents apiece to ride. The railway ran until 1938.

America's first true roller coaster opened at Coney Island in the late 1800s. Located by Brooklyn, Coney Island became New York City's playground in the 1850s. Coney Island offered city dwellers sunshine, surf, and shore. Visitors also found shows, food (the hot dog was invented here), carousels, fortune-tellers, and guess-your-weight booths.

LaMarcus Adna Thompson, a Sunday school teacher from Ohio, believed that roller coasters could provide more wholesome fun for young people than Coney Island's bars and beer gardens. Thompson also thought the Mauch Chunk switchback railway's success showed that roller coasters could be a good business. In 1884 Thompson built his Gravity Pleasure Switchback Railway at Coney Island.

Thompson's coaster held 10 passengers in a single car and rode down a gentle, wavy hill. Top speed was a rather calm 6 miles per hour. Nonetheless, Thompson's "gravity railway" became popular. At five cents a ride, the coaster earned an astounding $600 per day. Thompson paid the ride's construction costs in only three weeks.

LaMarcus Adna Thompson's Gravity Pleasure Switchback Railway of 1884 brought roller coasters to the United States.

The Father of Gravity

With the success of Thompson's switchback railway, Coney Island coaster competition heated up. Charles Alcoke added his roller coaster, the Serpentine Railway, late in 1884. He designed an oval track, so the ride began and ended in the same place. Six passengers sat in a car that looked like a park bench. They rode sideways so they could enjoy the view. At 12 miles an hour, Alcoke's coaster was twice the speed of Thompson's. In an issue of *Frank Leslie's Weekly*, a reporter said the faster ride was like "being carried away by a cyclone."

Phillip Hinckle added a chain lift to his 1885 Coney Island coaster, the Gravity Pleasure Road. The lift hauled cars up the first hill, saving his passengers a climb. Hinckle also seated riders facing forward. Soon Hinckle's and Alcoke's rides were hurting Thompson's business.

Charles Alcoke's Serpentine Railway, built shortly after Thompson's roller coaster, zipped along at the breathtaking speed of 12 miles per hour.

Thompson (above) built his finest scenic railway (left), in Venice, California, in 1910. Tracks took riders through tunnels, over "mountains," and past an ancient Egyptian temple.

Thompson wasn't nicknamed the Father of Gravity for nothing. His new coaster included his competition's improvements. Then he tossed in a few of his own. Thompson hooked cars together and created the first coaster train. He improved safety features, such as an automatic cable grip. This instrument grabbed the lift cable and stopped cars from rolling backward in an emergency.

Tunnels covered part of the tracks on Thompson's newest ride. Cars dove into the scary darkness and triggered that new invention, electric lights. The lights shone on painted murals of the Orient, mysterious grottoes, and historical scenes. Thompson named his new coaster the Scenic Railway and opened it in Atlantic City, New Jersey, in 1887. The ride was an instant hit.

Flips, Flaps, and Flops

Not all new coasters were successful, however. The first American looping coaster, or "centrifugal railway," appeared in 1888. Lina Beecher created the Flip-Flap and later sold the ride to Captain Paul Boyton. Boyton set up the Flip-Flap at his Coney Island attraction, Sea Lion Park. Riders climbed into two-passenger cars. There were no seat belts, so riders wedged themselves in the best they could. The cars swooped down a 30-foot drop and whipped around the loop. Unfortunately, the force of the ride made passengers uncomfortable. Many riders complained of back and neck pains. The Flip-Flap flopped.

Edward Prescott tried a looping coaster, named the Loop-the-Loop, in 1901. The loop was a teardrop shape, not a true circle like the Flip-Flap. The design reduced the problems that plagued the Flip-Flap. Only four passengers could ride at once, however, and not many of them wanted to repeat the trip. Low ride capacity—the number of paying customers who could ride in an hour—doomed the Loop-the-Loop.

Like the Flip-Flap, the Loop-the-Loop was a flop.

The Golden Age

Roller coaster construction exploded during the 1920s, an era known as "the Roaring Twenties." Fueled by city trolley systems, amusement parks popped up all over the country. Park owners constructed larger and scarier roller coasters to attract more customers. Riders thrilled to 1,500 wooden coasters, or "woodies," by 1929.

Coney Island added a legendary woodie called the Cyclone in 1927. The coaster featured an 85-foot initial drop. Advertisements at the time called it "The Most Fearsome Coaster Ever Built." Around 75,000 people showed up on opening day. The Cyclone was so popular it paid off its $100,000 cost in just one year.

Several wooden roller coasters built during the 1920s are still running. At Kennywood Park near Pittsburgh, Pennsylvania, you can find three. Built in 1920 for $50,000, the Jack Rabbit features a 70-foot, double-dip drop. The 1924 Pippin is on the other side of the park. This ride was remodeled in the 1960s, creating the heart-stopping Thunderbolt. The last drop of the Thunderbolt is the first drop of the old Pippin. Kennywood's Racer includes two tracks running side by side. Opened in 1927, the Racer is the oldest original racing coaster in the world. These Kennywood coasters usually appear in lists of favorite roller coasters.

The Racer at Kennywood Park in Pennsylvania

Coney Island's Cyclone (right) *brought these words to the lips of Emilio Franco* (above): *"I feel sick."*

The Cyclone even received credit for a miraculous medical cure. In 1943 West Virginia coal miner Emilio Franco lost his ability to speak. Doctors could not find a medical reason for his condition.

In 1949 Franco rode the Coney Island Cyclone with his cousin. Franco stumbled off the coaster and spoke his first words after six silent years: "I feel sick."

The Great Depression of the 1930s and the world war of the 1940s ended the Golden Age of roller coasters. Millions of people lost their jobs during the Depression. Families spent money on food, not on trips to amusement parks. During World War II, wood and rubber were vital for the war effort. These materials were not available to maintain roller coasters, and many began to decay.

The economy improved after World War II, but people did not return to amusement parks. Cars and new highways let families create vacations far away from home. When people stayed home, they watched free entertainment on television. Cities grew and surrounded many amusement parks, bringing traffic and crime problems.

The number of amusement parks fell from around 2,000 in 1920 to 368 in 1948. Over 1,000 scream machines fell silent and were torn down. Many of the amusement parks that stayed open into the 1950s were dirty and sometimes unsafe.

A New Era

Filmmaker Walt Disney changed that in 1955. Disney became interested in making a place where families could enjoy themselves. His creation, Disneyland, was the first theme park. Instead of slapping down rides here and there, Disney planned the location of each ride with care. Disneyland's attractions fit in with the themes of various "lands," such as Frontierland and Tomorrowland.

As television grew more popular and as cars and highways become more common, local amusement parks lost their appeal for many Americans.

Disney opened the Matterhorn Bobsleds at Disneyland in 1959. Using his film *Third Man on the Mountain* as inspiration, Disney re-created a smaller version of the Matterhorn, a famous Swiss peak, in his park. It seemed natural to include bobsledding as part of the attraction. Cars for the ride were made to look like bobsleds. They raced through a 147-foot-tall replica of the famous mountain.

The miniature peak was constructed from 2,175 pieces of steel, no two the same size. This was the first modern steel roller coaster. Unlike previous wooden coasters, the Matterhorn Bobsleds' cars had nylon wheels running on tubular steel tracks. Despite the popularity of the Matterhorn and the advantages of steel construction, Disneyland's ride did not kick off a boom in new coasters.

The Matterhorn Bobsleds ride at Disneyland in Anaheim, California, was the first modern steel roller coaster. Its looks owed a lot to an earlier wooden coaster—L. A. Thompson's Scenic Railway in nearby Venice.

Steel coasters *(above)* now make up over 50 percent of all operating coasters. The steel tracking and nylon wheels offer a smoother ride. Steel coasters also cost less to build than wooden ones, a big plus for park owners. Steel tracks allow the creation of more terrifying coasters. Tracking can be twisted and shaped into loops and corkscrews.

It took an old-fashioned woodie to get people excited about riding giant scream machines again. In 1972 at the Kings Island amusement park near Cincinnati, Ohio, a new coaster opened. The Racer wasn't innovative like the Matterhorn. It was a large wooden ride that recalled the Golden Age of coasters in the 1920s.

The public soon fell in love with the Kings Island Racer. Theme park owners across the country added wild new coasters made of wood or steel to attract customers. The number of major coasters in the United States grew from 147 in 1979 to 164 in 1989, to over 200 in the late 1990s.

The scream machines are screaming again.

The Racer at Kings Island, near Cincinnati, Ohio, kicked off a new Golden Age of roller coasters that shows no sign of ending.

Chapter 3

These Dogs Don't Bark

Most of this roller coaster's circuit can be seen from the top of the first hill.

Wood or steel, winding or straight, roller coasters come in all sorts of sizes and designs. Despite their differences, coasters share common parts. You would find these parts on a typical roller coaster.

A complete roller coaster ride is called a **circuit.** Viewed from above, the circuit of a roller coaster can look like untied shoelaces.

Riders climb on the coaster at the loading platform and get off at the unloading platform. Most modern roller coasters combine these two platforms into one. Passengers enter the coaster from one side and exit from the other side. This speeds up the loading process. The loading/unloading platform is located in the station.

23

Three kinds of wheels—road wheels, upstop wheels, and guide wheels—keep roller coasters running on the track.

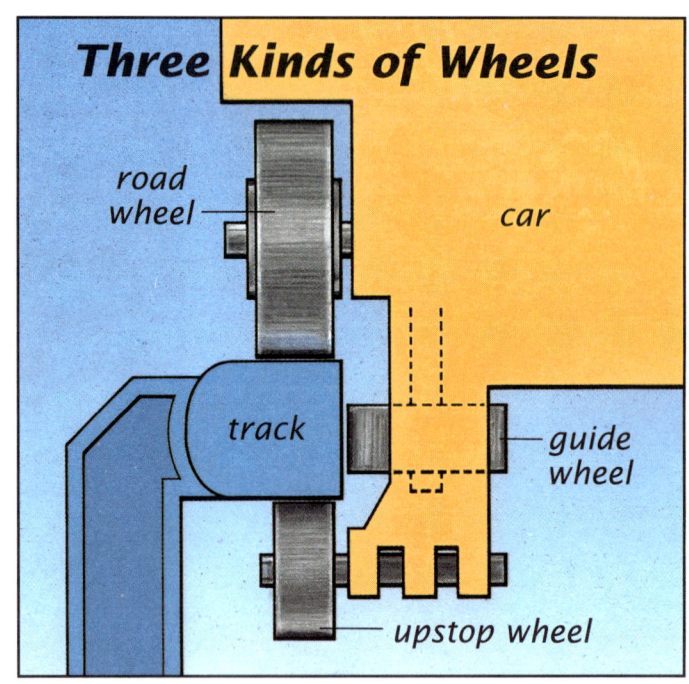

Two or more cars linked together make a train. Ride operators use the dispatch panel to dispatch, or send out, the loaded trains from the station.

Up to 15 passengers ride in cars. The cars use three different types of wheels. The road wheel runs on the top of the rail and carries the car. The upstop wheel (sometimes called the under-friction or underside wheel) operates under the rail. Invented by John A. Miller in the early 1900s, it keeps the car from jumping off the track. Another wheel running along the side of the rail is called the guide or side friction wheel. The guide wheel stops the car from sliding off the track sideways.

Restraint devices such as over-shoulder bars help keep riders in their seats during loops and turns.

Restraint devices, such as lap bars and over-shoulder bars, hold riders in place. These first appeared in the early 1900s, when the Dayton Fun House and Riding Device Company invented the automatic lap bar. Shoulder restraints, headrests, and divided seats are standard equipment on modern coasters, particularly those that loop.

Many safety features and other devices used in modern roller coasters can be traced back to one man, John A. Miller. At the age of 19, Miller was hired by LaMarcus Thompson to work as chief engineer on Thompson's new Scenic Railway. Miller showed a talent for improving old designs and coming up with new ideas. He eventually patented over one hundred roller coaster devices and improvements. Three of Miller's coaster designs from the 1920s—the Pippin (now the Thunderbolt), the Jack Rabbit, and the Racer—are still thrilling riders at Kennywood Park in Pennsylvania.

The very first American roller coaster, Thompson's Switchback Railway, had none of the safety devices later pioneered by Thompson's chief engineer, John A. Miller.

Riders hear a "clack, clack, clack" on the way up. The noise comes from ratchets (sometimes called antirollbacks). Ratchets are steel bars with claw shapes cut into them. They are installed on the track. If a train starts to roll backward down the hill, ratchet dogs under the cars catch the ratchets. That stops the train.

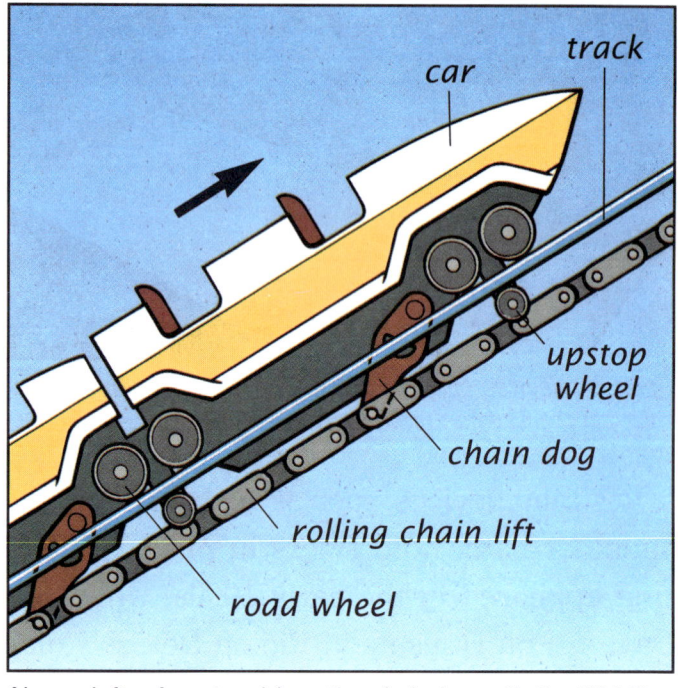

Above, left: *A motor drives the chain beneath the lift hill.* Above: *Chain dogs under the cars grab the chain lift, pulling the coaster up the lift hill. At the top of the hill, the chain dogs are released, and the coaster train is ready to go!*

All Aboard!

The train leaves the station and is hauled up the first hill, or **lift hill**. Under each car is a piece of metal called a chain dog. The chain dog grabs a rolling chain called the chain lift that hoists the train up the lift hill.

At the top of the chain lift, the train hurtles down the first drop. This is the highest and most exciting drop of the ride. Most first drops slope down about 50 degrees. How much is that? Stand a pencil straight up and down on a table. The pencil's slope is 90 degrees. Stand another pencil next to the first. Pretend these pencils are clock hands pointing to 12:00. Move the second pencil toward the tabletop. Stop when the two pencils look like clock hands at 12:05. The second pencil's slope is about 50 degrees. That's a pretty steep slope!

The slope on the first drop will send a train a long way, but some roller coasters also use booster wheels. These motor-driven wheels are put in a flat section of track. Booster wheels give the train an extra push along the track, often helping to bring the train into or out of the station.

Usually, the steep slope of the first drop isn't apparent to riders until the train reaches its highest point. These riders still don't know what lies ahead.

Brakes, chain lifts, or other devices divide roller coaster tracks into blocks. Only one train can be in a block at a time. This is a safety measure. If, for example, one train stops on the track, the coaster's safety system performs a setup. Other trains are stopped in their blocks to prevent one train from ramming another.

Putting on the Brakes

The most important safety system is the brake system. Originally the ride operator pulled a brake lever at the station or in the car itself to stop the train. Sometimes the operator didn't use enough muscle. The train overshot the station, and the passengers got a free ride! Modern roller coaster brakes are pneumatic, powered by air pressure, not by muscle. They're also located in the middle of the tracks, not on the cars. The brake controls are at the station.

Coasters use two types of brakes to slow or stop trains. The trim brake slows or stops the train at preset locations. It is used if the coaster is running faster than it should, since a too-fast train wears tracks rapidly.

Brake controls are located inside the station.

This train will soon pass over brakes located on the brake run, a section of track located just outside the station.

The second type of brake is the station brake, which slows the train as it enters the station. This brake is located on the brake run, a flat section of track as long as two or three trains. It is located just outside the station. Many brake runs are covered to protect the brakes from rain. When brakes are wet, it's harder to stop the train.

Computer controls direct the brakes to open and close.

Computers control braking systems. Electronic sensors built into the tracks trace the trains. Then computers process the information and control the brakes, if needed.

Some coasters also use computers to weigh a loaded car. The computer adjusts the space between cars based on the passengers' combined weight.

Board the train, get dispatched out the station, and climb the lift hill. It's time for a science lesson.

These riders are speeding down the first drop. They're also taking off on a rapid lesson in the science of motion and gravity.

An electronic sensor located alongside the track sends information back to the computer.

Chapter 4

Curves, Corkscrews, and a Few G's

Roller coaster tracks spiral and turn. Sophisticated computers control safety and speed. Coasters run with chilling names such as Magnum XL-200, Mindbender, or Thunderbolt. Despite all that fancy stuff, roller coasters use natural laws of motion and **gravity** described by Sir Isaac Newton back in 1665.

Motion and gravity laws are part of physics, the study of matter and energy. Two basic kinds of energy are part of a roller coaster ride. Hauling the train up the lift hill, like winding a watch spring, gives the coaster stored-up energy, called **potential energy.**

Sir Isaac Newton

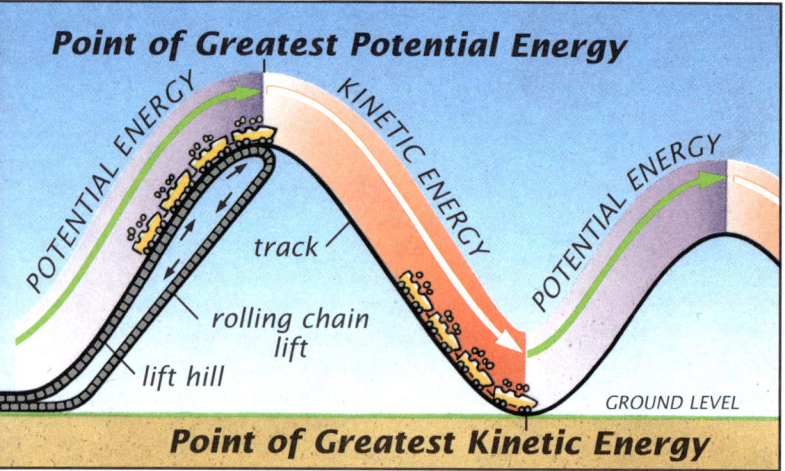

The cars crest the hill and slip down the slope. The train speeds up the closer it gets to the ground. The coaster's potential energy is changing into the energy of motion, called **kinetic energy**.

The coaster swings between potential energy and kinetic energy throughout the ride. The train has potential energy going uphill and kinetic energy going downhill.

The amount of potential and kinetic energy shrinks as the ride continues. That's because the roller coaster gradually runs out of **momentum.** Momentum is the force or energy gathered by an object's acceleration. For example, the faster a bike is pedaled, the more momentum it has. If the rider stops pedaling,

A roller coaster swings between potential and kinetic energy.

the bike coasts because of momentum. A coaster builds momentum rushing downhill.

In a typical roller coaster ride, the first drop gives the coaster enough momentum for the entire ride. If the train runs out of momentum, it runs out of "gas." The coaster won't have enough power to climb a hill and will get stuck in a valley. Since that is rather embarrassing, the first hill must be the highest one.

Heading over a hill, this coaster's potential energy turns into the energy of motion, also called kinetic energy.

What a Drag!

The coaster can never go as high as it does when leaving the first drop because of two forces called **friction** and **drag.** Two objects rubbing together cause friction. For example, bike hand brakes produce friction. Squeeze the lever, and rubber pads press against the bike's wheels. The friction created between the unmoving pads and the moving wheel slows the bike. Moving through the air makes friction, too. This is called drag.

Friction and drag slow any object in motion, including a roller coaster train. The coaster's wheels rolling on the track create friction. The train moving through the air creates drag. Friction and drag slowly drain the train's kinetic energy and momentum. If friction and drag didn't exist, all the coaster's hills could be the same size. Since friction and drag reduce the coaster's energy, each hill needs to be smaller than the one before. Even if the coaster's brakes failed, friction and drag would eventually slow and stop the train.

Besides the brakes, the only things that will slow this roller coaster train are friction and drag.

All roller coasters use a common power source. That is gravity, the force that pulls everything toward the earth. Gravity gives objects—and people—weight. When you stand on a scale, the scale's numbers show how much gravity is pulling on you.

Gravitational forces, known as **g forces,** tug at people constantly. Normal earth gravity exerts a g force of 1. Astronauts float around at 0 g's. Jet pilots black out at 10 g's.

On a roller coaster, g forces decrease as the train goes down a hill and increase as the train climbs. When the coaster train shoots up a hill, gravity has other ideas. It wants to pull the train toward earth. Riders feel this battle through changing g forces. Positive g forces make riders heavier. Negative g forces make riders lighter. If a rider weighs 60 pounds at 1 g, he or she would weigh 180 pounds at 3 g's.

Most roller coasters pull no more than 3.5 g's. Average riders find higher g's simply too scary. The Texas Giant, a typical modern coaster at Six Flags Over Texas, pulls 2.7 g's. That may sound tame, but it's almost as many g's as astronauts feel during a Space Shuttle launch. Three coasters outside the United States generate more than 6.5 g's. These nail-biter coasters are the Mindbender in Canada, the Dreier Looping in Germany, and the Moonsault Scramble in Japan.

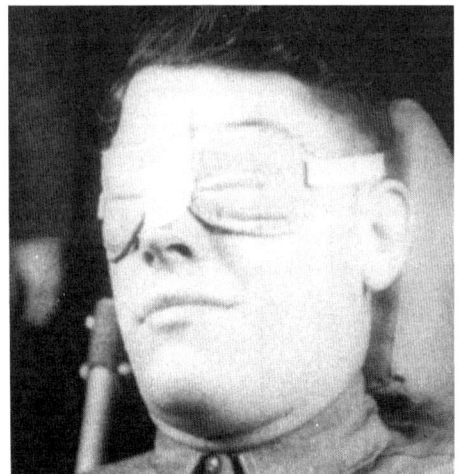 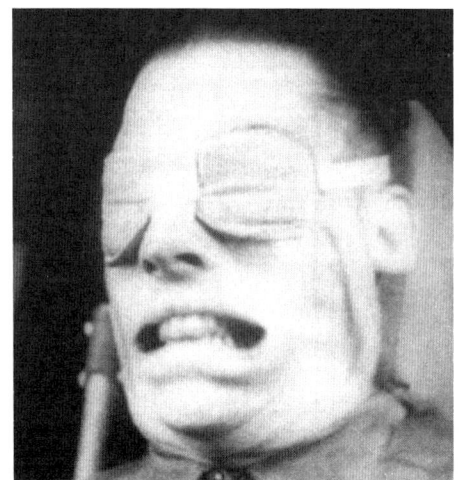 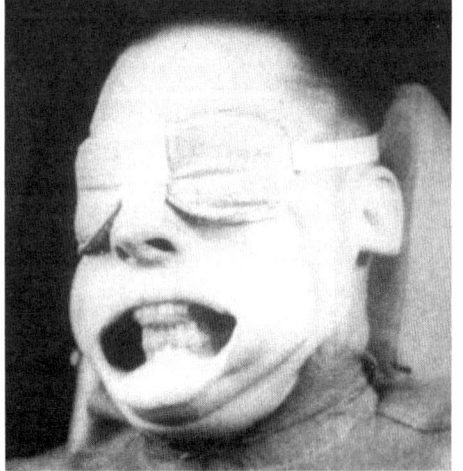

An astronaut undergoes testing at a g force of 1 (left), *of 5* (middle), *and of 10* (right).

Superman the Escape in Valencia, California, makes riders feel weightless—at 0 g's—for 6.5 seconds.

G forces rapidly drop as the train rounds the top of a hill and heads down, or when it reaches the top of a loop. Riders may briefly experience 0 g's, although coasters generally don't go lower than .2 g. If a rider weighs 60 pounds at 1 g, his or her weight is reduced to 12 pounds at .2 g. The sudden shift from positive g's to negative g's lifts riders from their seats. Coaster fans call the effect "airtime."

Roller coaster trains obey the laws of gravity and momentum. They also follow the law of **inertia**. Inertia states that an object will keep moving in a straight line unless an outside force stops it. For example, a ball rolling across the floor will continue to roll until it runs into something or until friction and drag slow it. The coaster's tracks control the train's inertia. Imagine a train that is not locked onto the coaster's tracks. The cars speed toward the top of the hill. The tracks turn down. The train's inertia keeps it going straight into the air. That might be a thrilling ride...*once.*

This blur of a roller coaster pulls 4.3 g's.

If a roller coaster ride makes things look like this on the outside, imagine what things must look like inside your body.

Revisiting Lunch

G forces affect your stomach, ears, and joints. As g forces increase, your stomach is squashed flat. The effect is like squeezing a plastic ketchup bottle. The ketchup squirts out the spout. Your stomach, like a bottle, may send the ketchup on a return visit, along with the cheeseburger and fries.

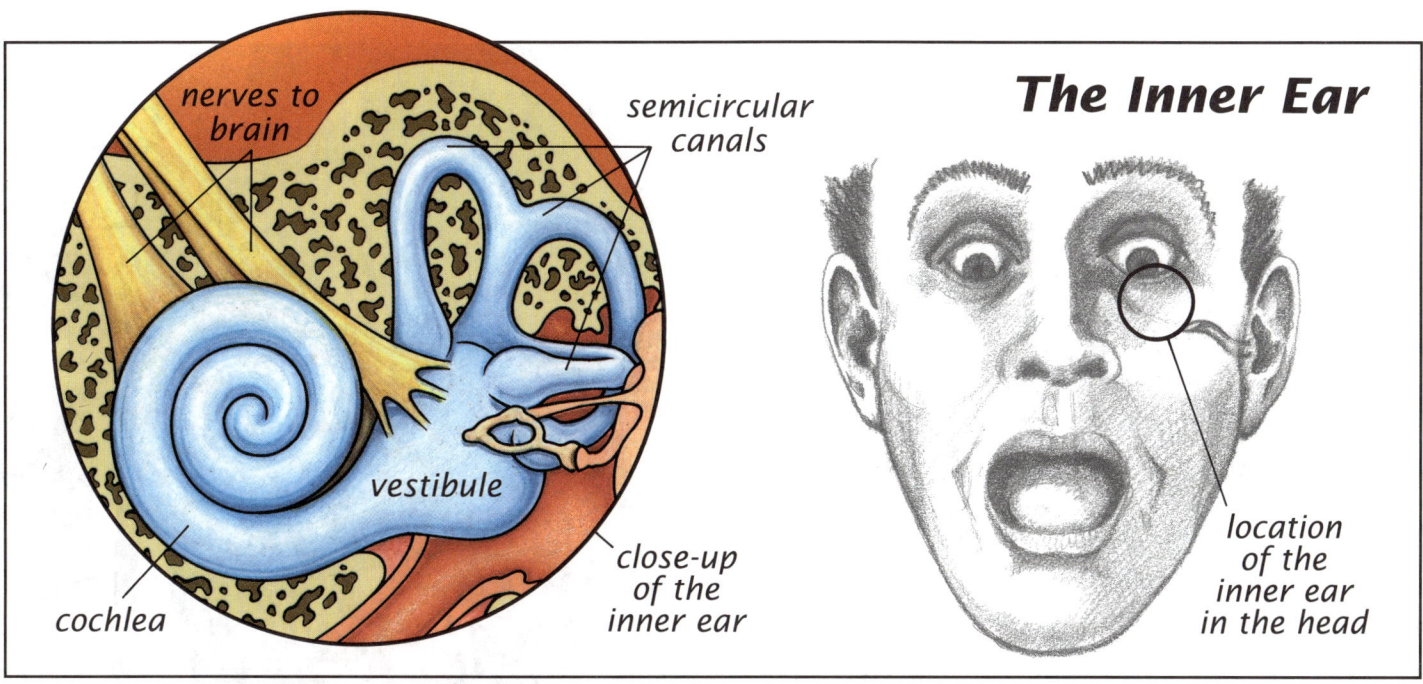

Fluid within the semicircular canals of the inner ear moves rapidly during a roller coaster ride, sending confusing information about body position to the brain.

On a roller coaster, you usually hear screams from fellow riders. However, the ear is not just the organ of hearing. The inner ear holds three semicircular canals. They tell the brain about balance and about how the body turns in space. The canals are filled with fluid. When you change position, the fluid in the semicircular canals changes. This causes nerves to send new body position information to the brain. During a coaster ride, the fluid in the semicircular canals sloshes around. The churning fluid, combined with the changing, blurred landscape, can lead to dizziness or motion sickness.

Your joints are also sensitive to the coaster's gravity changes. Muscles and joints contain **proprioceptors.** They keep track of how the joints and muscles expand and compress. As you zoom around a coaster circuit, you may stiffen and relax your body in ways different from normal activity. This sends more disorienting information to the brain.

Twists and Turns

Some coasters travel faster than people can react. Imagine that you're riding in a fast car coming up to a sharp turn. You'd probably automatically brace yourself in your seat. It's tough to do that on a roller coaster because of speed and unexpected turns. The result is a jostling but thrilling ride.

Coasters don't just go up and down on straight tracks. Sooner or later, the trains have to turn. Turns on roller coasters are usually **banked,** or tilted at the outer edge, for a more comfortable ride. Without banked turns, riders would bang into each other like boxes sliding across a seat when a car turns a corner. A slow coaster train does not need a steeply banked turn, but a high-speed train requires a steeply tilted curve.

Turns on a roller coaster are tilted up at the outer edge to allow for a smoother ride.

When a roller coaster goes through a turn or a loop, **centripetal force** acts like an invisible seatbelt for riders. Centripetal force holds a moving object in a circular path. For example, the friction between a car's tires and a road provides the centripetal force needed for the car to turn a corner. During a rainstorm, a slick road may not provide enough centripetal force. The car may continue its natural straight path and skid off the road.

The teardrop shape of this looping coaster lowers the g forces exerted on riders to a safe and comfortable level. Centripetal force keeps riders in the cars, even when the track turns them upside down.

Because its designers did not understand centripetal or g forces, one of the earliest looping coasters, the Flip-Flap of the late 1800s, was unsuccessful and dangerous. Modern looping and corkscrew coasters take advantage of materials that early coaster designers didn't have—nylon or polyurethane for wheels and tubular steel for tracks—to create safe and comfortable loops. By using a teardrop shape (an idea first used in the Loop-the-Loop coaster) instead of a true circle, designers reduce the extreme g forces that made the Flip-Flap flop. Engineers working in the 1970s found that the Flip-Flap's circle shape exposed riders to nearly 12 g's. Modern teardrop-shaped loops cut that number to 6 g's or less for a safer, smoother ride.

Well-designed banked turns and loops balance the centripetal force and g forces in a typical roller coaster ride. These forces are directed through the rider into the seat. Riders stay safely planted in their seats—even on the scariest curves, corkscrews, and loops.

Riders may climb off a coaster thinking about the fun they've had. But they've also received one wild lesson in science.

Riders on this roller coaster don't know what to expect next—except that they will be scared, and scared safely.

Chapter 5

Engineering, Psychology, plus a Little Courage

Modern roller coasters represent complicated engineering. Designers and engineers may produce thousands of pages of blueprints, layouts, and plans for a single coaster. They make Styrofoam and wooden models of each coaster before it is built. They also check—and double-check—the forces exerted on riders, cars, and tracks.

A good designer thinks about more than just engineering, physics, and safety. The goal is to create an unforgettable experience. Once on board, riders fall into the designer's clutches and can't escape until the train pulls back into the station.

Designers start with the new coaster's audience. Will the riders be primarily families or thrill seekers? Families generally prefer a milder ride than do thrill-seeking roller coaster enthusiasts.

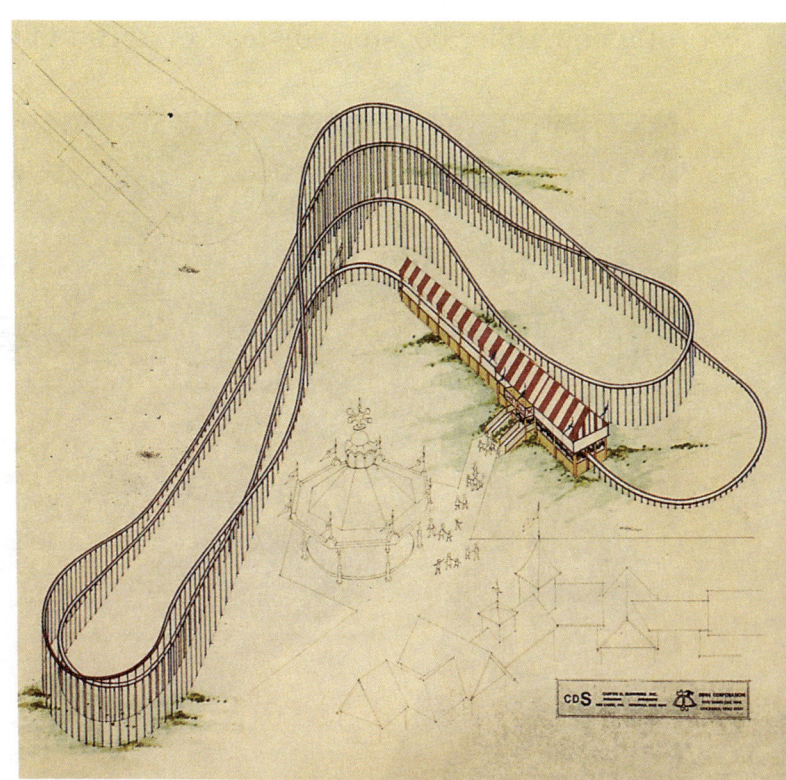

A designer's layout for a new coaster

Getting the Lay of the Land

The size and geography of the ride's site are also important. Engineers must know the location of possible obstacles, such as lakes, rocks, or power poles. The position of underground utilities, such as gas lines, also affects design and construction. Some obstacles can be worked into the ride.

At Adventure City, a small California amusement park, a large tree grew in the path of a new roller coaster. Instead of uprooting the tree, designers sent the coaster's track up and over a branch!

Roller coasters require a lot of land, particularly for banked curves. Busch Gardens's Kumba coaster in Tampa, Florida, sits on a full three acres (14,520 square yards).

If a designer has to shoehorn a coaster into a smaller area, the turns must be squeezed onto less land. The result can be jolting and uncomfortable turns.

Designers and engineers must check out the site for a new roller coaster.

Designers solve space problems creatively. Knott's Berry Farm, California, faced a space problem with their Jaguar coaster. There wasn't enough open space available for the ride, so the coaster crisscrosses public walkways and weaves through the Mexican Village theme area. It even shoots through the loop of another coaster.

Designers had to fit the Jaguar at Knott's Berry Farm in California into a small space.

The fit is so tight on the Great Nor'easter at Morey's Pier in New Jersey that very tall passengers can't ride. The coaster weaves around a water slide.

Designers sometimes incorporate natural terrain into a roller coaster. Kennywood Park's Thunderbolt, for example, does not start with a lift hill. The train leaves the station, then plunges into a ravine. The lift hill is near the middle of the ride.

How do modern roller coaster designers like their work? John Allen, whose Racer at Kings Island sparked a coaster revival, described his job this way: "You don't need a degree in engineering to design roller coasters; you need a degree in psychology—plus courage." Veteran coaster designer Ronald Toomer summed up coaster design in a 1992 interview. People in line should "feel like they're going to die," Toomer said. "Hey, they want to feel that way."

A designer uses a computer to "build" a roller coaster ride.

Simulations, Scribbles, and Surprises

A new coaster is first "built" on a computer. The computer's simulation figures out the amount of g forces generated by each foot of track and by every twist and turn. If the forces are too high, designers modify the track and recalculate.

The hills, dips, and curves of a coaster's blueprints may look like crazy scribbles. But a thrilling coaster should be as well thought-out as a gripping adventure movie. There's a big start, followed by a few thrills. Then the designer may throw in some straight track so riders can catch their breath. A variety of hills and turns can be added for more thrills and chills.

Opposite page: *The designers of the Coney Island Cyclone knew how to give riders thrills and chills. Creaking timbers add excitement to this classic coaster.*

The designer may turn a hill into a "double dip" by flattening the slope halfway down. Perhaps a very steep drop, called a "slammer," could be added. How about a "hoopty-do"? That's a sharp left turn followed by a sharp right. The designer can add more airtime with "speed dips." Coaster trains take these hills at high speed.

A favorite design trick is called *fine del capo*, which means "end of the head." The coaster shoots directly toward a support beam but ducks under it at the last minute. You may have the distinct feeling you're about to lose your head. That's why this trick is also known as a "head chopper." Not to worry, though. Roller coasters use a minimum clearance of nine feet between the car and the overhead beam.

Different building materials can add to the thrills. Creaking and clanking wooden coasters seem a little more primitive, and perhaps more dangerous, than their steel cousins. Some modern coaster fans prefer wooden coasters to steel coasters for that very reason.

Inside Disney's Space Mountain, electric lights add to the sense of motion.

Several methods can add the illusion of greater speed. Whizzing past trackside objects, such as posts or trees, is one way. Keeping the train close to the ground, in what is called a gully coaster, makes it seem faster. Special lighting effects, tunnels, and darkness can also be used. Disney's Space Mountain runs in the dark with projected stars moving in all directions. The ride *feels* much faster than its top speed of 28 miles per hour.

Tinkering with the chain lift can increase dreadful anticipation. Sometimes a designer will make the trip up the lift hill slower than necessary, just to increase riders' fears. Hiding what lies around the next bend is another fear-heightening technique. When building outdoor coasters, designers use trees, foliage, or tunnels to hide or screen the rider's view. Hiding a drop in a dark tunnel is always good for a scream or two.

The Thunderbolt at Kennywood Park, a gully coaster, zips along close to the ground, giving riders the illusion of greater speed.

You can make even the tamest ride more thrilling by using the tips for a scarier ride below.

Top Ten Tips for a Scarier Ride

Want an even scarier roller coaster ride? Coaster enthusiasts offer these tips:

1. The front car feels faster. It is also best for a good view and for a feeling of floating.
2. The rear car gives more airtime.
3. If you ride in the rear car, lift your feet and look up as the train crests a hill. This gives you a feeling of a free fall.
4. During the ride, close your eyes briefly and then reopen them. Do you feel confused?
5. Look backward to get that dizzy feeling.
6. To get that sick feeling, look to either side when the train goes through a loop.
7. Lift your feet as the car crests a hill. That increases a feeling of weightlessness.
8. Ride a coaster in the rain. The water makes the tracks slicker and the ride faster.
9. Another good time for a fast ride is at night, after a rain. Many people think the tracks are slickest then.
10. Ride an outdoor coaster during hot weather. The heat thins the grease on the coaster's wheels, increasing the train's speed.

Insert Tab B into Slot A

Once the design work is complete, steel track sections are constructed at the factory and shipped to the amusement park in pieces. The coaster is assembled at the park. If everything goes well, the sections fit snugly together.

The new coaster is tested thoroughly before opening to the public. Sandbags, each weighing about 150 pounds, "ride" the coaster first. Water-filled mannequins also sit in for real people. Next, park workers volunteer to ride.

Before you take a seat, sandbags ride a new coaster to test it for safety.

At the amusement park, steel track sections are put together like parts in an enormous model.

Then it's your turn. You reach the head of the line. Riders spill out of the train. Some are laughing. Some stagger a little. Those two look green.

You take a seat. Nothing to worry about, you think. People have been doing this sort of thing for hundreds of years.

The over-shoulder restraints and lap bars clamp down. The coaster is designed for speed and safety, you tell yourself. The car's special wheels and computer-controlled brake system keep the train on the tracks. The banked turns, loops, and hills all direct the g and centripetal forces to keep you in your seat. You clutch the lap bar anyway. Why are your knuckles white?

You try to smile bravely. The designers want you to think that the coaster is dangerous, you tell yourself. This will be fun! Really! Honest!

The cars lurch out of the station. The chain grabs the first car and hoists the train up a steep hill. "Clank! Clank! Clank!"

For the thrill of a lifetime, there's nothing better than a roller coaster ride.

A Coaster Spotter's Guide

Roller coasters come in many flavors, but they can be grouped into basic types. Use this guide to identify the different kinds of coasters at amusement parks.

A *classic* coaster, or coaster classic, is a different thing to different people. Members of the American Coaster Enthusiasts use the term for a wooden coaster that harkens back to the Golden Age. Lap bars allow for plenty of airtime. Seats aren't divided, so riders slide from side to side. There are no headrests to block the view. And riders can choose where they'll sit. Other people use the term *classic coaster* to describe any wooden coaster.

An *out and back* coaster's circuit is a long oval. The train leaves the station, travels through a turnaround curve, and returns to the load/unload platform.

Classic (above): Giant Dipper, Santa Cruz Beach Boardwalk, Santa Cruz, California
Out and back (right): Starliner, Miracle Strip, Panama City, Florida

Racer coasters feature parallel tracks. Two or more trains leave the station at the same time and race each other.

Figure eight: Leap the Dips, Lakemont Park, Altoona, Pennsylvania

The track layout of a *figure eight* looks like the number eight. The tracks make left and right turns and cross each other.

Racer: Gemini, Cedar Point, Sandusky, Ohio

A *suspended* coaster's train runs under the track, instead of on the track. The cars can swing and sway.

Suspended: Ninja, Six Flags Magic Mountain, Valencia, California

An *inverted* coaster's train also runs under the track. But unlike a suspended coaster, the inverted coaster's cars do not sway or swing.

Inverted: Montu, Busch Gardens—the Dark Continent, Tampa Bay, Florida

Passengers ride a *stand-up* coaster standing up instead of sitting down.

Shuttle loop: Montezooma's Revenge, Knott's Berry Farm, Buena Park, California

Shuttle loop coasters have a single track. On most, the train shoots out of or is pulled from the station. It flips through a loop, then climbs a high, steep slope. The train stops at the top of the slope, then zooms through the loop and the station...backward. On the other side of the station, the train climbs another steep slope, stops, then returns to the station.

Stand-up: Shockwave, Paramount's Kings Dominion, Doswell, Virginia

Trackless: La Vibora, formerly Avalanche Bobsled, Six Flags over Texas, Arlington, Texas

Enclosed: Space Mountain, Walt Disney World, Orlando, Florida

Trackless coasters were originally called flying turns. Cars that look like bobsleds zoom through a deep trough. These rides first appeared in the 1920s, with wooden troughs. Modern models use steel.

An *enclosed* coaster runs inside a building.

A *twister* coaster's track is a tangle of turns. Riders can't figure out what's coming next.

Twister: Texas Cyclone, Six Flags AstroWorld, Houston, Texas

Glossary

banked: sloped or inclined upward from the inner to the outer edge of a curve or turn

centripetal force: the force that is needed to keep an object moving in a circular path

circuit: the complete path of a roller coaster

drag: the force produced by air when it flows over a solid body. Drag slows movement.

friction: the force coming from two surfaces rubbing against each other

g forces: a measure of the amount of gravity acting on a person or an object

gravity: the force that pulls objects toward the center of the earth

inertia: the principle that states that an object in motion will keep moving in a straight line unless stopped by an outside force

kinetic energy: the energy of an object that comes from the object's movement. In contrast with potential energy, kinetic energy is energy that is being used.

lift hill: usually the first hill, a roller coaster's lift hill must also be the highest. A chain on the lift hill pulls the coaster to the top.

A pair of true roller coaster fans celebrate their wedding on the Cyclone at Coney Island.

momentum: the energy that comes from the force and speed of an object's movement

potential energy: an object's stored energy. Potential energy depends on an object's position or state.

proprioceptors: nerve receptors in the body's joints and muscles. Proprioceptors tell the brain how the joints and muscles expand and compress.

Great Places to Look for More on Coasters

Check out these books on scream machines:

Cartmell, Robert. *The Incredible Scream Machine: A History of the Roller Coaster.* Fairview Park and Bowling Green, Ohio: Amusement Park Books, Inc., and Bowling Green State University Popular Press, 1987.

*Silverstein, Herma. *Scream Machines: Roller Coasters Past, Present, and Future.* New York: Walker, 1986.

Throgmorton, Todd H. *Roller Coasters: An Illustrated Guide to the Rides in the United States and Canada, with a History.* Jefferson, N.C.: McFarland & Company, Inc., Publishers, 1993.

*Wiese, Jim. *Roller Coaster Science: 50 Wet, Wacky, Wild, Dizzy Experiments about Things Kids Like Best.* New York: John Wiley & Sons, Inc., 1994.

*An asterisk indicates a book for young readers.

For information about the American Coaster Enthusiasts, or ACE, write to:

American Coaster Enthusiasts
P.O. Box 8226
Chicago, IL 60680

Daring riders try out a Coney Island roller coaster, in about 1900.

On the Internet, look for these Websites:

http://www.chebucto.ns.ca/~ak621/CEC/CEC.html
Take a look north of the border at the official Website of Coaster Enthusiasts of Canada.

http://www.coasters.net
A Website loaded with photos and information on coasters and amusement parks around the world

http://www.fmcg.com/jmiller/
This Website is devoted to the life and work of coaster designer John A. Miller.

http://www.lifthill.com
The Lift Hill is packed with photos and information on coasters past, present, and future.

Index

Aerial Walks (1817), 11
Alcoke, Charles, 15
Allen, John, 44
American Coaster Enthusiasts, 50, 55

banked turns, 38, 40, 49, 54
Beecher, Lina, 17
Boyton, Captain Paul, 17
brakes, 28–29, 30, 33, 49: pneumatic, 28; station, 29; trim, 28

Catherine the Great, 9
centripetal force, 39, 40, 49, 54
classic coaster, 50
Coney Island, N.Y., 14, 15, 17, 18, 19
Cyclone (1927), 18–19

Dayton Fun House and Riding Device Company, 25
Disney, Walt, 20
Disneyland (Anaheim, Cal.), 20, 21, 46
drag, 33, 54

enclosed coaster, 53

figure eight coaster, 51
Flip-Flap (1888), 17, 39
France, 10, 12
Franco, Emilio, 19
friction, 33, 54

g forces, 34–35, 36, 39, 40, 44, 49, 54
gravity, 31, 34, 37, 54
Gravity Pleasure Road (1885), 15
Gravity Pleasure Switchback Railway (1884), 14, 15
gully coaster, 46

Hinckle, Phillip, 15

ice sledding, 9–10
inertia, 35, 54
inverted coaster, 52

Jack Rabbit (1920), 18

Kennywood Park (Pittsburgh, Penn.), 18, 25, 43
kinetic energy, 32, 33, 54
Kings Island (Cincinnati, Ohio), 22, 44

Knudsen, Richard, 12

Loop-the-Loop (1901), 17, 39

Matterhorn Bobsleds (1959), 20–21, 22
Mauch Chunk, Penn., 13
Mauch Chunk switchback railway, 13, 14
Miller, John A., 24, 25
momentum, 32, 33, 35, 54

Newton, Sir Isaac, 31

out and back coaster, 50

Paris, France, 10, 11
Pippin (1924), 18, 25
potential energy, 31, 32, 54
Prescott, Edward, 17
proprioceptors, 37, 54

racer coaster, 51
Racer (1927), 18, 25
Racer (1972), 22, 44
roller coasters: decline, 19–20; design and engineering, 41–46; history, 9–22; kinds of, 50–53; looping, 17, 39, 40, 47, 49, 52; parts of, 23–30; physics, 31–40, 41; safety, 8, 11, 41, 49; steel, 21, 23, 45, 48, 53; testing, 48; wood, 21, 22, 23, 45, 50, 53
Russia, 9, 10
Russian Mountains (1804), 10–11

Scenic Railway (1887), 16, 25
semicircular canals, 37
Serpentine Railway (1884), 15
shuttle loop coaster, 52
stand-up coaster, 52
suspended coaster, 51

Taylor, J. G., 12
Thompson, LaMarcus Adna, 14, 15, 16, 25
Thunderbolt, 31, 43. See also Pippin
Toomer, Ronald, 44
trackless coaster, 53
turns. See banked turns
twister coaster, 53

wheels, 21, 24, 27, 33, 39, 49: booster, 27; guide, 24; road, 24; upstop, 24

Photo Acknowledgments

Photographs and illustrations courtesy of: Andy King: front cover, pp. 21 (right), 23, 24 (bottom), 25 (left), 26 (left), 27, 28, 29 (both), 30 (both), 39, 49; Paul L. Ruben Archives: back cover, pp. 9, 14, 16 (both), 19 (right), 25, © Richard Cummins, pp. 1, 2–3, 7, 32, 33, 35 (both), 40; Corbis-Bettmann, pp. 5, 20, 31; © Betty Crowell, pp. 6, 48 (bottom left); © Paul L. Ruben, pp. 8, 18, 22, 41, 43 (bottom right), 44, 46 (bottom right), 48 (top right), 50 (right), 51 (top and bottom, right), 52 (left), 52 (top right), 53 (bottom right); Independent Picture Service, pp. 10, 11; Linda Hill Collection, Paul L. Ruben Archives: p. 13; Archive Photos/American Stock, p. 15; Library of Congress, p. 17; New York Times Pictures, p. 19 (left); Walt Disney Productions/Paul L. Ruben Archives, p. 21 (left); Laura Westlund, pp. 24 (top), 26 (bottom right); Archive Photos, pp. 31, 34 (all); © Warren Stone/Visuals Unlimited, p. 36; © John Elk III, p. 38; © Busch Entertainment Corp./Paul L. Ruben Archives, p. 42; © Knott's Berry Farm, p. 43 (top right); © Richard B. Levine, pp. 45, 54; Walt Disney World/Paul L. Ruben Archives, p. 46 (top left), 53 (top right); © Buddy Mays/Travel Stock, p. 47; Santa Cruz Seaside Company, p. 50 (left); Cedar Point®, photo by Dan Feicht, p. 51 (left); Kings Dominion/Paul L. Ruben Archives, p. 52 (bottom right); Six Flags Over Texas/Paul L. Ruben Archives, p. 53 (left); Alexander Alland Sr./Corbis-Bettmann, p. 55.

Nick Cook, a frequent visitor to Disneyland and other southern California amusement parks, is a roller coaster fanatic. When he isn't riding the rails of a coaster train, Cook works as a speech pathologist and lives in Huntington Beach, California. *ROLLER COASTERS, or, I Had So Much Fun, I Almost Puked* is his first book for children.